E. Lynn Alexander

COLLAPSE PRESS

FIND ME IN THE IRIS © 2022
by E. Lynn Alexander
Print ISBN: 978-1-7352669-3-0
Ebook ISBN: 979-8-218-01122-2
Collapse Press

All rights reserved. No part of this book may be reproduced without permission of the author. For inquiries, please contact info @ collapsepress.com

FIND ME IN THE IRIS

E. LYNN ALEXANDER

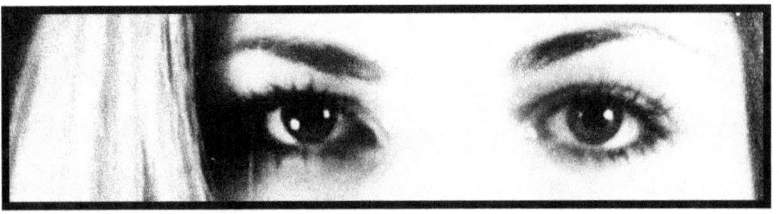

In Memory of
My Mother

A pile of copper.
When copper was the color
That loved her.

CONTENTS

Honey. Wheat. and Figs.
The Urgent Traverse
Bottles of "Were"
Bottles of Disease, Never Seen
Frogs with Glowing Eggs in their Bellies
Cabinet of Grief
Odd Jobs
A Jar I Call Anonymous
Between Shouting and Silence
Observing a New Gardener
Full of Crow
Auburn. Mother. Monsters.
The New Medusas
Gravity, For the Catching
The Codpiece King
Typewriter Keys We Eat
Blue
Daughter
The Ganglia Grid
The Witch of Me, I Keep in the Velvet
    of My Bones
Find Me in the Iris

Bottles of "were"
Of regret.

Something she said.

It stuck with me.

What will the grief of me teach you?

HONEY. WHEAT. AND FIGS.

Mother, blue. Hue from her wings.
Honey. Wheat. And Figs.
A pile of copper
Amniotic. Ewer.

Horizon. Blues of oceans.

Sky, pooled to pupil.
Dilation
Pulled to vanish

As to a black hole.

THE URGENT TRAVERSE

We pool. Commune
With our moon-mother
Chasing, drapes of linen
For the throne

We step out from the shadows
In found forms
We reach
Across the needing
We search
With our bones

We reach
We lay logs
Across the road

We rise. We form. We fall.
We meet the water.
We cross, as current
East.
West.
We ebb.

We stretch, through latitudes
Retreat.
And return.

We crest. We surge.
The urgent
Traverse.

We find the silences in storms
We rise in their eyes.
In the iris-

Mother. Blue. Blues of ocean.
Sky. To the pupil.
Pulled to vanish

As to a black hole.

We reach
Across the needing
We search
With our bones.

We trench. Beneath us, boring.
Into Earth

Coring from her crust
We pull
From the land

We set apart: A pillar
Obelisk
A monument
For the shore.

Banded with the ages
Striping of chronologies
Striations of extinctions
We measure the slivers
Of women. Men.
Them. Civilizations.

Eras of words.
The slice of war.

Set apart, beside the ocean
Pillar. Testament.
Monument
To our destruction

Obelisk
We've made this
For our moon.

We pool. We commune.
With our
Moon-mother.

We crest. We surge.
East. West.
We ebb.

The urgent
Traverse

We reach
Across the needing

We search
With our bones.

BOTTLES OF "WERE"

Bottles of "Were"
Of regrets.

Something she said
That stuck with me

What will the grief of me teach you?

Bottles of "were"
Stacked up. On a shelf.
Behind Shoulds. And Shames.

And samples of disease
We've never seen.

Words. Dissolving in formaldehyde.
Tongues. Of Other.
Bottles. Holding younger selves.
Other selves
Who "were".

Selves who "were",
Now their labels
Going brown.

Time ticks.
Selves stuffed down.
Time ticks.
They've formed a gallery
Of "used to be"

Honey. Wheat. And Figs.
Piles of copper.
Time ticks.
Linen skins.
Mouths that drowned.
Time ticks.
Their lips fixed
in their final sounds.

Time ticks.
Seven. Stillborn specimens.

Who they "were"
Stuffed down
To bloat and yellow
In their brines.

Eyes. Open. Orbs of "were"
Hazel. Brown. Blue.
Every iris
Slivers of the Pillar.

When once their lashes fluttered
For life
Twitching
To exist

Feeling heavy in the want
The lids
Slid down.

Now the lashes float, colloidal,
Beneath the buoyant bulbs
They become the sludge.

In found forms, we reach
Across the needing
We search
With our bones.

Bottles. Corked. And closed.
Women. Mothers.
Suspended
In their ages
Selves, the slurry sediment
Their labels going brown.

Faces. Slipped.
From alabaster heads
Tilt at the neck
Left to bob there in their bottles.

They speak to me.
These specimens-
They bob against the glass
Their eyes find me

They settle on my face
I can't look away.

One. By. One.

One. By. One. They say:

What will the grief of me teach you?

BOTTLES OF DISEASE, NEVER SEEN

Bottles of "were" and "shoulds"
and "shames'
Bottles
Of "might have beens"
Bottles of disease
never seen

Time. Ticks.
Time. Ticks.

Bottles of bees
We've eaten

Bottles of honey
Holding queens.

FROGS WITH GLOWING EGGS IN THEIR BELLIES

Specimens. Bobbing
Beneath their stoppers.

Particle flecks, held up to the light
I see tadpoles

Larvae. Eggs. Algae.
Mother-moon
Alchemy

I see metals of industry
Poisons.
Run off from the lawns.

Toxins. Plastics. Bag Phantoms.
The ghosts
Of Wants vs. Needs

The war we lost.
The earth grieves
In rust
And beads
Attached to teeth.

Bottled frogs, with glowing eggs
In their bellies
Keep asking me

What will the grief of me teach you?

CABINETS OF GRIEF

I have poured them from my head.
Wet with the yellow
of collecting.

They trickle down my neck.

I'm dispensing
apothecary brews

Spells for youth
None of them
Could cure you

Mother-moon

I am your collector.
Curator.
Cabinets of grief.

Masks in the gallery

I keep these bottles
Stacked up high
Hundreds of rows
deep

ODD JOBS

I am a chemist. I mix up tinctures
from their spleens.
I patent. I peddle.
I sell grief.

I am a doctor. I take up scissors
to my sisters
I sew up their bellies
I take teeth.

I am an artist.
Taken brushes to their pigments
Taken thickness
From their mud.

From hair, I weave
Tapestries.
I am Creator.
I make forests
From memory.

I am a priest. Pin women
to my trays. I dissect them.
I display their hands
I verify stigmata
I name saints

I am a plastic surgeon. Scalpel scraping.
Gristle bits. Sculpting silhouettes.
Sizing meat.

I am a butcher
Thoracic
I probe cavities.
Snapping sinew from the ribs
Selling silverskin
Suet.
Haggis full of acids.

I am a factory farmer.
I keep women with the beef.
Their milk becomes cheese
in copper lockers.

I am a geologist.
I have a volcano of women,
stacked.
Their lava stopped.

I am the inspector
For the government
I keep spreadsheets.
I read policies.

I have shaken your jars, held them up
Checked their purity
Checked their color
Against an institutional guide

My rubric is a bulletin
Released by an Administration.
A bureau
I grade you
For the industry.

I am a regulating entity
I am a commissioner

Of safety.
I am bureaucracy

I have crash tested prison walls
hurling bottles to the floor
Like snow globes

My pitcher arm is authority
calibrated by a machine

I have turned them upside down,
Sediments disturbed
I shake them
I time them
I evaluate performance
See if they can flip
Check if they can self-correct

And I make lists.

I am police. I have taken them out with my badge
I am judge. Jury.
I examine their bodies.

Popping bones out of sockets,
their dull tensions
I measure

Tensile strength
and bitter. brittle. elastic.

I report on their breaking points

I invent scarcity.
I trade in the art
Of wanting.

I make molds for machines
Cast you, anew

I mass produce
Pressed flesh
I categorize
into sizes

I categorize their eyes:

Hazel
Brown
Blue

I find my mother's iris
And I hold it up to mine

I try to peek

They take away

My keys.

A JAR I CALL ANONYMOUS

I make them into piles
Over and over
To be built again
Like piles of nails and screws
For a house

Genesis. Metals.
Gears for machinery.

There's always something
Left over. Or missing.
In building.

There are holes
Where our hearts
used to be

I fill spaces
With seeds

I keep a jar
I call "ANONYMOUS"

She is bits

From the heap.

BETWEEN SHOUTING AND SILENCE

Limbo. Lunatic. I've been stuck this way.
Between shouting. And silence.
Quiet
But angry eyed.

Watching the world outside
The reel
Frames flipping
I suspect
Subliminal messaging.

I've been stuck this way
Like I am riding by in a car,
Face against the glass.

Moving slowly down streets
Watching people
on the sidewalks.

Going in different directions, some with babies
Some oblivious.
Some in a rush.

Some standing around
Some shouting.
Some silent.

We are stuck
This way.

OBSERVING A NEW GARDENER

It is the first Spring in her new home, and every new shoot is a mystery. There are guesses about the trees, predictions, hopes for summer fruit.
"Hope", she says, "is a seed."
She pats her swollen belly.

She is a different woman in Winter.
As we are, as we learn
To be.
She is a different woman in a decade
In two. In three.
The crone we fear
Can bring relief.
She is a different woman in Winter.
As we are, as we learn
To be.

There are bulbs. Anonymous.
Underneath.
Like eggs, they wait
To be.

They wait. They have learned
About reaching out
too soon.
there is no retreat
for the green.

Gardening is a balance
of patience
and decisions.
Freedom
And control.

When they bloom
When they brown

When to wait
When to prune

When to nurture
When to split

We learn- there is brutality
In frost.

And the cutting and plucking
Pinching and thinning
For their own good.

There are decisions.
Who gets covered, or moved inside
There is scrutiny.
Who among them
Are drought resistant?
Desired, by deer?

Spring breaks catharsis.
The dirt warms.
In tension like an orchestra
In every breath, held.
The green waits
On the crows.

FULL OF CROW

The world is full of crow,
Wings against the sky.

We step out from our shadows
In found forms.
We search
With our bones.

Anticipation,
I have worn you as my blister.

When
Has been the question

It has stretched
Me taut.

Time. Ticks.
Time. Ticks.

Bottles of bees
We've eaten.

Bottles of honey
Holding queens.

"I ask this one thing: let me go mad in my own way." (Electra)

AUBURN. MOTHER. MONSTERS.

I keep specimens of gore.
Samples of disease.
I wittle. I carve.
I make scrimshaw ships.
Home decor. Nautical themes.
Taken tusk.

I grab faces and hands
Mannequins from stands
Glossy photos to ripple
In formaldehyde.

I have taken fractured pelvic pieces
Through their teeth
"Baby birthing hips"
Slid
From their spines.

I have taken their hair
Piled wet locks by the fire
where they dried

Felted pelts. Matted knits. Meshed wire.

I have taken black and blonde
And auburn. mother monsters.
Clipping them
to strips.

To my mother,
Chopping copper
Dropping snakes
to the floor

Swept snakes, that crept
And wrapped around tongues.

Tongues of men
Now dead cement.

Copper and cement
Gone gray

My auburn. mother. monster.

Gorgon copper.

I have chopped you.

Honey. Wheat. And figs.
A pile of copper.
Amniotic. Ewer.

Dead cement. A pile of copper.

When copper was the color

That loved her.

THE NEW MEDUSAS

Bottles. Selves. Stuffed to fit.
Pushed in with sticks.
Inside
They hiss.

Within, regrets
Fill the vessels
Burdens
That bulge.

Within, their skins
Become cement
Wrinkles. Etched in stone.

They sink. They take the shapes
They have reduced to.
Their fingers have taken to prune
They do not plump.

They bob, mouths open
Lips shifting. Hissing.

Specimens, gone gray.

Their rings slide away
Their jewels offer nothing
but rust.

GRAVITY, FOR THE CATCHING

"There is something instead of nothing. There is something. Do you hear me?"
"No."

I have poured from these pitchers.
Taken gravity, for the catching.
My shitshow of metal and debris
My sidewinding car
I am driving
I am arriving
I am rinsing
And repeating.
Disease.

Stained streets
The streams
Of rust

Water is doing

What water does.

It seeks

Its low.

TO THE CODPIECE KING

The temple door is bruised.
We women
Kicked it in.

The metals have cooled.
The nails still hold him.

I am collecting specimens again.
Bottles, lined up by the door
Bottles for her. For them.
Archive
Of "were"
And "when"

I take singing from the sirens
Bring the blood from the ships
Their token teeth. And tusks.
Appropriated. Apparatus.

I take the babies from the men
At the mast
Men, strapped and crying
Ears ringing
Around the Codpiece King.

I snatch them. Pull their hands from their ears.
I scream
With the fury
Of all of us: "HEAR ME"

TYPEWRITER KEYS WE EAT

HEAR ME
HEAR THEM
HEAR US
HEAR WE

I have carried these typewriter keys
We stole back
to the beach.

Back to the beach
For my sisters
To feast

I bring stolen whiskey
I wash their feet

I take sirens from their bottles
And return them to the sea
With fingers pulled
From the cement
We tap the keys

Time. Ticks. Tap. Click.
Tap. Click.
We tap the messages of mothers

I type my question to the sea:

What will the grief of them teach me?

BLUE

I am being replaced
Board by board
Beam by beam.
I become the building that I wasn't.

I am down to the studs
Of what I was
I am rough, wound-toothed.
I have holes
where the screws
used to be

There are new spaces. Empty.
Within me. Things were taken
from in between me

I am vertical. Weight bearing bones.

I am witness.
I inhabit
And I hold
What I was.

I hold up a house
I do not own
There is no deed
With any mention
of me.

I have no key.

I am a skeleton
Holding up a body
I am underneath an architecture
I did not design

The weight
is binding

I am being replaced
board by board
And beam by beam
Beams
From my beginning
Are gone.

In the prying
In the pulling
I will be there for the last

I will be there
Then I won't be

Just like that.

They say our cells are replaced every seven years,
That in time,
We are variations

Persons
Who we weren't.

Board by board

We become the babies

Who we weren't.

They say our cells are replaced
They never know
if they will be the last
to be tasked

with this

configuration.

*Somewhere, a mother
with invisible stitches
sits up.
"Something was taken from me."*

"You should rest," they say.

"Try not to speak."

*I am infected. I have pockets full of rocks.
I don't hear you.
I am begging for the beetles.*

I am begging for the beetles to eat me clean

*To the vines of my mother
I cry: make rot of me.*

(From *The Shouldspeak Disease*)

DAUGHTER
(FROM *PROLOGUE TO MARIAMNE*)

Wet left. Weeping skin.
To leave as steam.

When faces leave their stations
They grow strange
Covered. In the film of things.
Ancient ashes. Film of shame.
Their hands had fanned
at things that vanished

Flames, now obliged
of all things body
Becoming black
The ash, corporeal. Black.
Black began to lap
across her skull.

She waited. The drape of linen
never came.
No shroud. No shrine.
Dense beneath herself
The orbs were soon
consumed

Left describing in her mind
without eyes
She became a scribe
without text
Woman without implements
Fingers without instruments

And silent in the dampers
They sat back
And watched her fingers
Growing furious

In the clasp of arms that bellowed
their hands
would fan her hair
to ash
To black
To vanishing

Soon her dust
Was in their rugs.

Erased of all things. Base.
And cranial.
Woman, burned mute
Frozen furious
In the death chew.

Erased, she was.
Of time. Of place.
Of name.

Swaying in the heat, loose limbed
as a wild hose

To turn to jerking spells of taut

Seized, they

Watched her fingers
Growing furious

Black, to vanishing
Their hands would fan her hair.

Soon her dust
Was in their rugs.

If she squatted

Only black

Would hit

the floor.

THE GANGLIA GRID

The cells conspire. Fuse. To unity.
They cluster at the brain, encased in new.
They surround it, as to a pit.
Like a rind. It crackles
as it cools.

They scuttle across the skull
They grow into continents.
They grow populations.
They communicate
with electricity
through the ganglia grid

They are given fire
For a time, there is novelty
Beauty.
They are given war.
They flicker at the fire like dancers,
cooling down.
Slowing in the minutes
Turning their backs
facing night, they leave the circle

Going dark. To other.
Forming countries. Nations.
Standing still.

The monuments begin.

The worshipping.
Gold gods, packed in tins.

Like mountains, they are pushed up from the land
Ice. Stones. Sand.
They rise
Casting shadows.

They rise up
As monuments
of sand

Never knowing if they will be the last
To be tasked

With this

Configuration.

THE WITCH OF ME, I KEEP IN THE VELVET OF MY BONES

Moon-mother, her cells form a nest
A saturated womb. For you.
Red from the fire, the heart
Beats blood out to the capillaries
Lush
Ripened. Like a plum.

Pearls in the pit-cling
Marrow. Mother.
The witch of me I keep
In the velvet of my bones.

We step out from our shadows
In found forms
We reach across the needing
We search
With our bones

We reach. We lay logs
Across the road.

We find the silences in storms
We rise up in the eye

I live apart from this

In the eye, I am alive.

FIND ME IN THE IRIS

In the eye
I am alive

I send the hue
For you to find me

Everything, Mother-moon
To the tides

The ocean pools
to the pupil
as to a black hole

Find me in the iris
in the blue
in the storm's eye
in the silence

We search with our bones
Mother. Moon. Blue. Hue.
Breath from her wings.

A pile of copper.
A plum.

Find me.

*We step out from the shadows
In found forms*

*We reach
Across the needing*

*We search
With our bones*

*A pile of copper. A plum.
Mother-moon.
Blue.*

Find me.

E. Lynn Alexander/2022

E. Lynn Alexander is a poet, artist, mother, maker of new from old...with a day job in a mission-driven nonprofit. She is the author of *The Shouldspeak Disease* from Naked Bulb Press and host/curator for various readings and events and founder of an arts collaborative.

Find out more at:
www.elynnalexander.com

SM: @elynnalexander

Thank you to my family, friends, and community who support creativity and connection.

Special gratitude: Paul Corman Roberts, Darrell Parry, Missy Church, Andrew J. Thomas, Moly Tov, Cleveland Wall, Chansonette Buck, Kim Shuck, Nancy Scott, Han Raschka, Richard Loranger, Karen Lillis, Chad Frame, and so many,many more. I hope you know who you are and that I appreciate you.

Also Available:

The Shouldspeak Disease

E. Lynn Alexander

Filament, Whose Time Inside the Glass
Has Passed

This disease leaves you alive
Until you aren't

Who you are gets thinner from within
Until you aren't.

It is figment
Until it isn't

The mind becomes a forgotten wire, naked
in the ceiling. A dead filament.

It was born into a bulb, to hum.

Filament
Whose time inside the glass
Has passed

Collapse Press- East and West- involves spaces. Pages, stages, the glow of a device... we are where we land. The goal is to create, share, sustain, include and amplify voices in these challenging times and promote community.

Please visit www.collapsepress.com for more information on books, events, and the monthly poetry series, The Friday Collapse.
#collapsepress #thefridaycollapse

www.ingramcontent.com/pod-product-compliance
Lightning Source LLC
Chambersburg PA
CBHW071254070526
44583CB00017B/2462